D1335391

NATURAL CAUSES

By the same author

Poems
The Pleasure Steamers
Independence
Secret Narratives
Dangerous Play: Poems 1974–84

Biography
The Lamberts: George, Constant & Kit

Criticism
The Poetry of Edward Thomas
Philip Larkin

Edited, with Blake Morrison
The Penguin Book of
Contemporary British Poetry

Natural Causes

ANDREW MOTION

Chatto & Windus

LONDON

Published in 1987 by
Chatto & Windus Ltd
30 Bedford Square
London WC1B 3RP

All rights reserved. No part of this publication may be
reproduced, stored in a retrieval system, or transmitted in any form,
or by any means, electronic, mechanical, photocopying,
recording or otherwise, without the prior
permission of the publisher.

British Library Cataloguing in Publication Data

Motion, Andrew
Natural causes.
I. Title
821'.914   PR6063.0892

ISBN 0-7011-3271-X

Copyright © Andrew Motion 1987

Photoset by Rowland Phototypesetting Ltd
Bury St Edmunds, Suffolk

Printed in Great Britain by
Redwood Burn Ltd
Trowbridge, Wilts

ACKNOWLEDGEMENTS

Acknowledgements are due to the editors of the following, in which
some of these poems have appeared: the *Literary Review*, the *London
Review of Books*, the *Times Literary Supplement*.

For Jan

Contents

PROLOGUE

The Dancing Hippo

In my country we are not good to animals.
A dog is a dog, however it might sit up
and beg, or run through fire; and a bear
riding a bicycle still wants to eat you.
I think you can see from my lack of illusion
I have some experience – so when I tell you
this story caused me distress, do not ignore me.

It's difficult, teaching a hippo to dance.
It takes for ever. They don't grow on trees,
and buying one meant that our modest circus
made do with a mothy lion for an extra year
and sold two singing seals. Then when she arrived,
our hippo, she ate like a creature possessed –
and the shitting! Continual diarrhoea, and her tail
dithering frantically, spraying it everywhere.
I have to admit, I wanted her sold at once,
or turned into curio waste-paper baskets.

But Nikolai reckoned she'd learn. Day after day,
and sometimes night after night, we'd hear
the Dance of the Sugar Plum Fairy (with whip
obbligato) twittering out of his tent, and *Move!*
Move! while he hopped around on the straw
as if it were burning his feet. A hippo able to judge
would have certainly thought he was mad; so it may,
I suppose, have been pity that led her to copy him –
a ponderous sideways prance, a shuffling reverse,
and a massive triumphant collapse (her curtsy).

Or that's what it looked like, at least,
the first time she danced for the public –
on a summer night in some one-horse place
we found by chance in the foothills,
with warm, mosquito-y, hop-smelling air blowing in
under the rolled-up flaps, and the people
caught in the spotlight transfixed by the prance,
reverse and collapse that we thought was nothing
but seemed to them like a miracle.

Maybe it was. For sure everyone loved her,
even when summer was over, and we returned
to perform in our permanent home, in the capital,
where they are used to marvels. On opening night
under the stars in the park, she excelled herself
in front of the President, rising at one time
(I think) on her chubby back legs for a second.
Afterwards Nikolai said she was not for this world
for long, and although he was right, his philosophy
wasn't enough to prevent the fire that burst
through her pen one night in the early new year,
and burnt her to death, from breaking his heart.

We live in a country where animals count for little,
as I have said. But I remember him stumbling into my van
after the flames were doused, and the huge carcass
had gone wherever it went, gripping my arm,
leaning close to my face in the yellow glare
of my rickety kerosene lamp, and saying
I know it was useless, of course, her dancing.
I know. Like everything else we do. But God above
it was beautiful. God! – or something like that.

NATURAL CAUSES

Bloodlines

1. Bro

We walked the way we had seen
our elders and betters walk
on their and their families' land:
with a head-back swaggering stride,
our hands stuffed deep in our pockets,

and pushed through a scraggy hedge
in the pewter afternoon light
to come to a spongy meadow
dotted with carious Cotswold boulders.
They'd told us to disappear

and discover the source of the Thames,
making us think we might find
a god stretched in a thicket
whose mouth was a massive O
spewing the river out into the grass.

But someone had stolen the god,
or maybe he never existed.
Instead we came to a patch
of stubbly reed where water
convulsed like a catch of mackerel,

and this, we supposed, was it.
We knew there was nothing to do
but quickly to match the pretence
of our head-back brazen approach
with a faked-up sense of arrival,

and stood there in silence a while,
watching the water swallow its tails.
Whatever came into your mind
was something you never said then,
and soon it was too late to ask

since a matter of days after that
I was parcelled away to school,
and took, as if it belonged to me,
the thought of the river collecting
the strength of a million ditches

hungrily under the ground,
emerging to shoulder through Lechlade,
and Oxford, and London, oily with prints
of tug-boats, and hurrying half-blind faces
peering from bridges, and giggling couples

throwing in twigs and watching them
wriggle from sight in curdling eddies,
and marvellous nineteenth-century walls
built right at the water's edge, so the eyes
of their gargoyles stare at themselves for ever.

2. Pa

On Christmas Day in the morning
my father and I snuck out
through the dripping bars of a fence
and walked the bounds of the parish

in that squished familiar round
(more like an egg than a circle)
we've walked for twenty years,
give or take an absence.

First stop, the blinding house
which used to be our home –
its stylish Regency white
splintered in bits by dead

elms sticking up through the view
so I never see it whole,
or quite believe it's real,
but feel I'm in the dark

like a man when a film begins,
who sees a house roll up
through a crazy blizzard of streaks
and a juddering number or two,

but finds when the story starts
that the house had disappeared,
and he's jumped across several years
(and whizzed across several fields,

and skirted one threadbare wood),
and come to rest at a grave
where after all this time
the words of my mother's name

are swarming with furry moss.
So many years without her
have taught my father to hide
in the gentle habits of someone

you might mistake for the gardener:
gently he rubs his hands;
gently he presses a dent
in the wiry green muscle

which ripples from under her stone;
gently he lodges upright
his dry jamjar of violets
suddenly whisked from a pocket;

and gently he turns away
to the dark, high-shouldered lane
which leads us up to the quarry.
We're clicking across the scree

that has dribbled from hills of gravel
when the sun breaks free from cloud
and strikes the flooded workings –
flashing along the water,

painting a row of larches
silver up one side,
making their spindly cobwebs
harden into targets,

and silhouetting a fisherman
calmly landing a fish –
a dead-weight, lustrous perch
with skin like a sodden log –

timing his catch so well
we think: it must be a trick.
And maybe it is a trick.
At any rate, we watch him

scoop the fish in his net
then swivel around towards us
as if about to speak:
You two look like people

looking out for something.
You don't think for a moment
it's the only time this fish
has fetched up on dry land?

It's lived like this for ever –
as long as I've been here,
a'hoiking out and bunging back.
Well; have you seen what you want?

He could have been shaking his fist
or waving us goodbye
when he'd stared for long enough
and hunched away once more.

We saw him collapse his net
like a black dishevelled stocking,
and slip the fish in the water
as though he were launching a ship

which sails along the bottom –
too deep for my father or me
to think it was worth our trouble
staying a second longer.

Scripture

Commonly called
The First Book of Myself

1. Now the Angel of Death rose against Austria, France, and the land of Russia, and fell from the sky over England, too – over Kent, London, and over the cities where people lived – and drove the young men into battle beyond the sea; and the women and old men, the halt, the lame and the weak it drove into shops and factories, onto the earth to farm it, and into the schools.

2. And it came to pass when the battle was ended, and people returned to their homes and livings, that in certain among the schools the old men looked on their work and it pleased them, and they did refuse the young men this work, and bade them go elsewhere.

3. And one of these schools was called Marrwell, Northants. And the children and boys there, after the battle was ended, found that a terrible strictness prevailed, and the rod was much feared, so the old men struck terror into the hearts of the children and boys.

4. And the Word of the Lord was abroad in the school, and there was much Scripture.

5. And I, Andrew, not eight years out of my mother's womb, was one of the children and boys who learned the Word of the Lord. And I lived in fear even at first, when I was put to study the First Book of Samuel, commonly called the First Book of the Kings.

6. And although God saw my innermost workings, yea, even where I was hid at the backmost part of the classroom, I wet my pants when I read me of Hannah's rejoicing, for it did make me think of the mother who was my own.

7. And lo, when the lesson was ended I was dried out, and no one did know of my wetness, and I did walk in the halls and out to the gardens smiling, for surely the Lord of Hosts was good, and this was a miracle.

*

At the end of a Sunday out
I lifted up mine eyes
to the dark glass front door
and saw my mother's face

gazing back at my own —
her long farewell look
more in pride than sorrow,
like Hannah's dizzy rejoicing:

My first, my lucky son,
I've hurried you out of home
although it grieves my heart,
knowing it's for the best.

May your enemies be confused
before you hear their tongues
utter a word against you,
and you, may you not be proud,

knowing the God of knowledge
is greater than all the thoughts
you have, or are likely to have.
The bows of the mighty are broken,

and those that stumbled are strong;
those that were full have now
hired themselves out for bread,
just because I who was childless

have you alive in the world.
Those who were poor are rich,
and those who once were low
are suddenly lifted up.

Sweetheart, do what you can
to keep the beggar and dunghill
out of each other's way,
so that the beggar may prosper

and sit on the throne of glory.
This is the least I can ask,
my first, my lucky son,
given your start in life,

and given that I'll be sending
the Airfix models you like
every week you're away,
and will post the first tomorrow.

*

Old Tosspot Pratt:
God-like, God-awful, granite-
jawed mask of authority,
headmaster and head of music.

I thought it best to be David —
a fair one, a smiley one, friend
to the world and its wife, sporting
the darlingest cowlick for miles

and flaunting it, even at Pratt.
From the way he marked my essay,
'Pretend you are Peter meeting the Wolf'
(me at his desk, his hand up my shorts),

the cowlick clearly had power.
Which was why, when his temper
snapped on the day that he dropped
and smashed his Haydn's 'Surprise',

the boy beside me whispered
Andrew! You help him — and why,
after picking the licorice splinters
up off the floor, I played for him

(well, in a manner of speaking),
tenderly bringing the needle down
on the record he offered (Ravel's 'Bolero')
as if I were soaking a sugar-lump

into a full cup of tea,
and seeing old Tosspot grin
before dandering back to my desk.
Religion, I thought, was easy.

*

Bilton Grange were philistines –
that had been gospel for years.
What did they feed their troops,
to make them so massive, and sour?

We ranged ourselves at kick-off
like puppies dreading a thrashing,
each hoping that someone else
would rise to meet the occasion.

The best we could do was Fort
(Fort T., that is, not F.) – and he
looked hardly more than a pygmy
at five foot eight and a half.

Out on the wing in the wind
(cold raising blotches like bruises
over my pitiful legs), I watched
Fort overwhelmed in the line-out

the first time we found touch,
and the ball fed out to their centres
so easily, deftly, and fast
they might as well have had magnets

strapped inside their wrists,
and we might as well have been flies
they breezily brushed aside
from then to the final whistle,

except that as Time drew near
my umpteenth totter to meet them
amazingly landed the ball
in my own stiff-fingered grasp

and I pelted towards their line
like a rabbit in flight from a shot,
and – though I might have been dreaming –
scored! 3–65! Goliath had lost his head!

*

But came a Sunday – the heart of a Famous Freeze.
The lake in the grounds was a sheet
through which – if you stood on the stepping stones,
peering down –
goldfish loomed and melted.
Out of bounds.

Out of bounds too was the swimming pool,
laid like sugary glass in its privet enclosure.

My afternoon's chance companion,
Jonathan,
pressed back the hedge and beckoned me in,
all innocence, simply because it was there.

Close up, it was not as we'd thought.
The glass was rucked – the pool whipped into waves
and frozen.
So when I skimmed a stone across,
instead of an iron tinkle and hiss
there was one crack and the stone stuck,
though its echo creaked and pinged for nearly a minute,
trapped in the liquid heart.

It was as though the face of a living thing
had been brushed by the wings of death,
and killed with its secret self laid bare –
a white, wild, bitter grimace
where we had expected steadiness, flatness,
the sheen of a distant summer.

It wasn't for this it was out of bounds,
but it was why, easing our way through the privet
and back to the school,
I carefully slid my hand into Jonathan's hand
and asked: *We won't tell anyone, will we? Are you my friend?*

*

The way old Tosspot exploded
when somebody turned a grass
and told him how they'd seen us
stooped to the magic ice
made us think the end of the world
was nigh, if not actually come.

He went to the pool himself,
even though darkness had fallen,
and measured our prints in the frost,
then bellowed us into his office –
Jonathan first, then me –
and never a sound escaped

through the studded green-baize door
to the one in the hall, waiting,
since both of us reckoned it right
to bow down and suffer in silence,
pretending that pain was dull
compared to the way each stroke

seemed to beat from our trousers
the wet sweet smell of wood –
faint, but surely surprising –
and telling ourselves the swish
of bamboo splitting the air
in a stinging fall from grace

left us with nothing to lose.
Back in the world we were heroes –
baboon-bottomed stars of the showers,
pioneers of the insolent slouch
at the gruelling seats of our desks –
and assumed to be plotting revenge

even if no one could see it.
When time enough (we thought)
had passed to make Tosspot ignore us,
we woke at one in the morning
and gingerly broke out of doors
with our dressing-gowns up round our ears.

All that we wanted to do
was simply to break a rule
no matter how scared we were –
and once round the lake at the double,

then up through the copse and in,
would have done it in half an hour

had not, mid-way through the copse,
the moon drifted suddenly clear
of a purple mountain of cloud
and shone on our upturned faces,
and seemed like the brilliant end
of an infinite tunnel of light

framed by flickering leaves,
and the words *Our father in heaven*
swelled into my head as a note
of voiceless, ravishing music
that no one could hear but me,
and which I could tell at once

was the note of absolute joy,
rooting me into the ground,
so it seemed a lifetime later
that Jonathan's voice was saying
You fool. For Christ's sake you fool.
They'll see us unless you buck up.

*

A fool, that was the thing to be,
a Holy Fool – perhaps for life,
perhaps for a term, or a week –
but always living inside the law,
as long as the law allowed me time
to please myself with my own devices.

Which was two afternoons a week —
enough, when spring came round,
to turn the copse to a wilderness,
and tell old Tosspot how sorry I was
for my grievous sins, and how I was
doing research for the school magazine:

The Birds of the Grounds. Did he know
of the flycatcher's nest in the cane-clump?
He didn't, but patted my head and smiled,
so I reckoned that I was forgiven,
and free to make myself scarce, become
someone who hid in the bole of a cedar,

loitered in shadows, spoke rarely,
and made the gateway to heaven
the apple-pip eye of the flycatcher
meeting my own for a second before
the cream wand of her tail flipped up
and shuddered down onto her eggs.

Those dreamy, dark afternoons
my head was lost in the clouds,
and it wasn't old Tosspot that finally
called me back to the world, more likely
Jonathan, thinking me up to no good,
and clambering into the cedar bole,

slipping his hand through my arm
to share whatever my secret was.
And if not Jonathan, then it was me
myself, thinking the way he smoked

pine-needles rolled in exercise-paper
made what I thought was heaven

seem drab, and the piercing eye
of the flycatcher simply a mirror
capable only of showing me how
I was clumsy, and huge, and strange,
and might one day rise up with a stone
and smash her eggs to a paste.

*

When Tosspot thought we were ready
he offered us God on a plate:
*Andrew, and you, Jonathan, you,
since you'll be leaving us soon
and be off to the wider world,
it's time you were getting confirmed.*

I knew that I'd left it too late
to take Tosspot's word for the truth,
but the lure of a quiet(ish) life
led me along to Class One
with Jonathan dreaming beside me,
sucking an Extra Strong Mint.

Tosspot had opened a window,
and rather than watching his face
I studied the way warm air
irresistibly dried off the fug
from the misty pane of glass
and thought: Does this mean what I think?

Does it mean what Jonathan thinks?
Though I knew if I turned to find out
Jonathan would have looked back
with one of his long-lashed winks
which closed and opened so slowly
he might have been falling asleep.

When I came to myself again
Tosspot was saying: *Confession . . .*
you'll have to confess, of course . . .
and almost the next thing I knew
was an altar rail under my nose
and a ghost reeking of mothballs

pushing a booklet into my hands,
whispering: *Listen, my son.*
In here you'll find some of the sins
you've already committed. I want you
to read them out when you're ready.
Now let us pray . . . In the blue light

falling like frost on the words,
on my clammy hands, I panicked
and read out the lot: *I have played*
with myself; been angry; insulted
my mother and father; been cruel
to helpless insects and animals . . .

hearing the silence stiffen,
then feeling a touch on my brow
– the cold caress of a shock –
and stumbling outside like a criminal

reeling away from his crime,
with the booklet gripped in my hand

as a file of repulsive evidence
I knew I must lose at once –
if only by leaving the path,
scrabbling a root-blocked hole
at the greasy foot of a yew,
and cramming it into the earth,

where the rain would surely rot it,
and mud destroy what I'd said,
even if after I'd gone
God delved underground like a mole
and scanned the pages in darkness,
learning my sins by heart.

*

1. Now it came to pass, on a day near the time we were due to depart for the wider world, and classes were almost over, and classrooms clean for parents to see, and rules slack, that a boy came in from the grounds with his clothes rent, and earth upon his head, to the library where I was killing time with a book, and said:

2. *How can you just be sitting there? He was your friend.* And vanished away to find old Tosspot, and tell him.

3. Now Jonathan, you were my friend, although our time was short, and we shared so little together. But

when it came to your death I was not at your side, and I never saw the place where you went, or even the van that took you.

4. O Jonathan, you were the first I knew to die, killed in our high, our secret places, by falling. How could you do it without me, climbing higher than ever we went in the cedar together, and falling.

5. I was left alone in the library, staring out at the cedar, and thought I could see you falling, splashed off the grainy plates of its branches.

6. I thought: this must be the time that God will appear to help me, and closed my eyes. What I saw was a golden coin flipped up in the air, winking and white as it caught the sun.

7. Lovely and pleasant you were in life, Jonathan, smoking the worst cigarettes in the world. Your courage was like an eagle's.

8. But the coin sank out of the sunlight, fallen, and I was alone in the library, clenching my eyes and seeing an empty space – empty, not even like vacant sky or deserted sea, but somewhere no wind might come, or rain.

9. How are the mighty fallen in the midst of battle! O Jonathan, thou wast slain in thine high places.

You Do, I Do

The Easter night they threw the bedsprings on the fire in
Argentina, what the bedsprings meant to you was food –
a giant grill. *Meat ladled from a barrow by two men*
with shovels, sweetheart, like the ones for pizzas:
veal and pork and lamb and beef and beef and beef.

Unknown to me, you hugged your knees, cross-legged,
and hoped the obvious and mad would come to pass.
It did: your charlady, for instance, and a taxi-driver,
lurching up to tango in a tango quite unlike the one we
know – 'Come Dancing', and all that. More like fucking

and a knife-fight rolled in one. You understand?
I do. I see you smile, half-skeletal and half-encouraged
in the juicy flames, and feel the eyes of strangers burning
on your mouth and arms and neck. The man beside you,
when the dance is over, thinks you'll be returning to his flat.

Our envies draw us further into love. Not only envies,
but they're part of it. And so, before your story ends,
you're propped up on one elbow in our crumpled bed
and asking me where I'd have been that night: alone,
I tell you, dozing in a frozen room – too tired for sleep,

and interrupted sometimes by that couple on the floor below
(those creaking shrieks, as though he might be winged
and lightly jumping on her from a wardrobe), sometimes
by the warning-buoy left groaning on the river streets away:
Don't come near me. Don't come near me. Don't . . . But why,

with so much water underneath the bridge,
should this concern us now? The instant I roll over,
press you gently back against the pillow,
stroke your hair out in its silky, spiky crown,
and stare into your face, I feel a stranger to myself

and all the lives I've led – like someone travelling,
whose boat has suddenly stood off a sunlit coast
with him on deck, who never saw these cliffs before,
or smelt this new-mown grass smell drifting out to sea,
but knows at once that he belongs here, and he's home.

Natural Causes

On the day that our boy was born
– the very same morning, in fact –
I left him beside his mother,
drove dizzily out of the hospital,
stopped at a grille-covered shop,
bought my paper, went home, and read –
after I'd shaved and bathed and dozed
for an hour or two in a stupor of joy –
the story of how an amusing, clever,
and now inconsolable man was one day
leading a more or less blameless life,
and the next day was crazy with fear.

He thought he was getting the flu.
He was put to bed, and four days later
escaped to be found in a cab
by his terrified wife, unable to think
what his address might be, or his name.
The hospital then, and every day since –
to discover his memory worked
just well enough to remind him
his memory no longer worked.
Give him the washing-up: no trouble –
each plate that he takes is the first.
Give him a long afternoon to sleep
in the sun-strewn hospital grounds,
and every three seconds he'll wake
to his utterly fresh despair.

Our son is a month old today,
and to celebrate woke us at 5 a.m.,
of course. A dingy, rain-spattered dawn,
and the three of us lay in our big double bed
with the pig in the middle between us feeding
with slobbery, wheezy, chirruping grunts.
Because it was early, because I was tired,
because I was almost lost to the world
with love for the boy, the thought of the man
with no memory came to me – as it had come,
I should say, hundreds of times before –
nervously, slithering into my mind
like a dog on a heavy painful rope,
yet lazily too, like a dog on a dusty day,
and stopped there: sinewy, not to be argued with,
bitter, but somehow banal, dragging behind it
other thoughts: *Those whom the gods . . .*
In the midst of life . . . The Lord taketh away . . .
What do we do to deserve . . . that sort of thing.

I've told you already, it's come to me
hundreds of times, the thought of the stranger
prowling his tucked-away hospital room –
which means I've encountered him often
each day in the life of our boy,
trying to compensate one with the other,
yet never quite able to bring them together,
except in a picture which hinges itself
in a triptych: the stranger on one side
stuck in a room with a single dazzling bulb,

who sees death laying its hand on his head
over and over again; in the centre, our boy,
a bundle shoved out to sea in one of those
hopeless wickerwork coracles under a furious sky;
and lastly ourselves – intelligent, petrified,
no way out of a cupboard of shiny steel with walls
which steadily squeeze together until we die.

Hare Lip

Like a genie escaping its bottle
this high-flying turbaned cloud
coagulates into a storm-head
and thunders down across Europe

unloading its piss-awful weather:
through suddenly-silver streets,
on clattering knots of birch
surprisingly warm from the sun,

on gates, on fattening streams,
and on a ribbon of polder
where in the thickening light
a hare grazes out in the open

then stiffens, then prods at the air
with its tremulous split upper lip,
then feels the rain on its back like a hand
rubbing its fur in the wrong direction.

*

I'm bending into your cot
at three or four in the morning:

sunk in a dream of food
your glimmering moon man's face

is still as death on the mattress,
except that every few minutes

a crinkling split-lipped smile
flickers and twitches and goes

like a butterfly haunting a twig
then battering off for no reason.

*

The hare on the polder trampolines
two foot into the air, and is running
as soon as it lands. It's only the rain,
but which of the creatures can know

rain isn't worth the effort
of desperate zig-zag sprinting
and spurting up salty earth
to try and find somewhere to hide?

Or failing escape, to pretend
that really you're something else
by freezing dead-still like this,
and becoming a perfectly normal

dock leaf late in the year,
the skiddering print of a horse,
an odourless loaf of dung, a clod
overlooked on a rutted sandy track?

Firing Practice

You knew you were lucky,
born all of a piece and born into peace.
So why were you seeing your father
off from the flagstone steps

wearing your *sweet little cowboy suit* –
distressed leather chaps
with grubby fringes – and him
in his real, steely-pressed uniform?

Once in a while he would take you:
Daimler sickness
swaying to Salisbury Plain,
and a rainy week-end of firing –

a privileged view from a rise,
which meant counting the seconds
from crash – *one, two* –
watching a tank half-hidden by gorse

silently stagger – *three, four* –
then the whump of its sad eruption.
Nothing connected with anything,
even then – not thoughts

with things, or you with him
(so what did it mean
to be lucky?)
no matter how hard you tried.

Twenty years on they're still at it.
You find yourself driving
each week over Salisbury Plain
to stay with the person you love –

and here, west from Stonehenge,
are those views you remember,
and tank-tracks scribbled on chalk,
their churned-up pastry mud

trailing off into nothing.
The tanks themselves are rare –
as if someone were trying to fool you
there mightn't be many –

but you know it only takes
lying in bed of a morning
(the children not yet awake
and none of the neighbours up)

to hear how resourceful they are.
Just when you might be
turning to face her (her eyes
still shut) and discovering

whether she wants you or not,
their firing will suddenly start –
a barrage of muffled thumps,
like someone heavy walking about

on the floor above (there is no
floor above), or slamming a window
in heaven. It never lasts long,
and at the beginning she said

It's one of those things, you know,
soon you won't notice it's there –
but you always do – the more,
in fact, the more time passes,

and sometimes you even imagine it.
You will be arm in arm, perhaps,
on that wind-swept, bare, slow-
climbing down overlooking the house,

and will think of a sound
which is faint
and yet somehow enormous –
enough to make grass seem to swerve

or trees to rattle their leaves –
and often they will.
When it ends you are stuck
with the thought you never expected

(because you were lucky)
and cannot quite feel is your own:
that what you are hearing as practice
is what will come true –

that soon you will die,
and not only you but this person
you love, her children, everyone else;
that no one prepared you for this –

no matter how early
you realised nothing connected
with anything, ever; that even
with her walking arm in arm,

and this place, which could be,
easily, anyone's favourite –
a watercress stream, a church tower
lightly shadowed by limes,

and the ploughland behind it
smudged with patches of chalk –
there's no one to save you now,
nowhere to hide in, nothing but hope.

EPILOGUE

'This is your subject speaking'

In memory of Philip Larkin

On one of those evenings
which came out of nowhere,
and one drink led to another,
and then to another,

at well past midnight
(rain stinging the window,
the gas fire burbling)
you suddenly asked me:

If you could meet one poet
– they could be living or dead –
which one would you choose?
Partly to please you I told you

Hardy. *Hardy*!
All he would say is: Motion?
One of the Essex Motions perhaps?
Then came your candid guffaw,

and just for a second or so
before I laughed too,
I heard the gramophone arm
we'd forgotten, still slithering

round and round on a record,
steadily brushing the label
and filling the room with a heartbeat:
bump; bump; bump; bump; bump.

*

49

East of Hull, past the fishdocks,
the mile after mile of raw terraces,
the bulbous, rubbery-looking prison,

fields begin scrappily – the first few
spotted with derelict cars and sheds,
but settling gradually into a pattern:

a stunted hedge; a dead flat expanse
of plough or tussocky grass; another hedge;
another vast expanse; and nowhere

under the leisurely, washed-out clouds
a single thing to disturb the rhythm
until, like a polaroid slowly developing,

there is the spire at Patrington –
a fretted tent-pole supporting
the whole weight of the sky.

I told you about it, thinking
your church-going days long gone
and anyway never spent here,

but *Yes*, you said. *The Queen of Holderness*,
and closed your eyes – seeing yourself,
I suppose, as I see you now:

the new librarian fresh from Belfast,
pedalling off one summery Saturday
(sandwiches packed in your pockets,

grey raincoat tied on the pannier),
finding the church, standing transfixed
by knots of lushly carved stone

in the nave's subterranean light,
hearing the tired clock, and feeling
that somehow no one had seen this before

or would do again, but nevertheless
convinced it would always be safe:
a shell as withdrawn as the mind,

where apart from the weary clock,
and wind rushing the leaded glass,
there was only the sound of your footsteps

clicking the wet green flagstones,
stopping, then clicking onwards again
as you finished your slow, irregular circle.

*

There was that lunchtime
you strode from the library
half-grinning, half-scowling,
onto the Great White Way.

Would you believe it —
(your head craned down,
your office windows behind
bulging with long net curtains) —

I'm reading the new Barbara Pym
and she says what a comfort
poetry is, when you're grieving
(but you were laughing):

'a poem by T. S. Eliot;
a passage by Thomas Hardy;
a line by Philip Larkin . . .' a line . . .
and think what I did for her!

*

One particular night
you were prowling in front of my fireplace
half an eye on your drink, half on supper,

and in the mantelpiece litter of postcards,
ornaments, bowls of odourless pot-pourri,
discovered a book-mark: 'Some say

Life's the thing, but I prefer reading.'
Jesus Christ, what balls! You slewed
round on your heel to the table

almost before your anger took hold.
Later, carefully pushing your glass
through the elaborate debris of napkins

and plates shoved any old how
(so it seemed you were making a move
in chess, or planning a battle):

You see, there's nothing to write
which is better than life itself, no matter
how life might let you down, or pass you by,

and smiled – a sad, incredulous smile
which disallowed everything you or anyone
listening then might have wanted to add.

*

. . . but then again,
I'm really not surprised to be alone.
'My wife and I have asked a crowd of craps'
and 'Keep them all off

put paid to invitations, I can tell you.
Though there was the time ——
(you made a fierce deleting bleep)
wrote: 'Philip, I've to be in Hull

from February second for a day or so;
I'll get to you at half past six.'
What could I do? I had a spare room
but no furniture. So out I went

and spent a fortune on a bed,
a bedside table, chest of drawers,
a looking-glass, 'that' (you grinned)
'that vase'. Anyway, he came and went,

and then a second letter: 'My dear Philip,
wonderful to see you looking well. Thank you
for your hospitality, and jazz, and drink,
and talk.' But not a word about the furniture.

*

Now look at this.
We were stooped side by side
to a glass display-case in the library.

Two poems in two days. 'Forget What Did'
and then 'High Windows'. No corrections!
Well, not many . . .

53

Your writing ran
across the dark reflection of your face
in lolloping excited lines. *Don't ask me*

why I stopped. I didn't stop. It stopped.
In the old days I'd go home at six
and write all evening on a board

across my knees. But now . . . I go home
and there's nothing there. I'm like a chicken
with no egg to lay. Your breath swarmed

in a sudden fog across the glass,
cleared, and showed you staring down
a second longer, reading through the lines

then straightening. *Not bad. But that's enough*
of that (one hand sternly guiding me away).
Come on. This is someone's subject speaking.

*

PS.
You know that new anthology?
The one that Mary Wilson edited
– the favourite poems of the famous?

Have you seen it?
Callaghan and Mrs T and I
all chose Gray's Elegy.
Why wasn't I Prime Minister?

*

The last place we met
(If I'm lucky I'll know
which is the last;

unlucky, I mean)
was the Nursing Home:
golden afternoon light,

a hot boxed-in corridor
tiled with lime-green carpet,
the door to your room ajar

and you in your linen suit
watching the Test on telly.
In the silence after applause

or laconic reports, your voice
was the cold, flat voice
of someone describing someone

they hardly knew.
Nobody's said what's wrong
and I haven't asked. Don't you.

Well I've nothing to live for,
have I? Christ, don't answer.
You'll tell me I have. Like seeing

Becker at Wimbledon, winning.
He looked just like young Auden.
That was good. I'm sure I'll die

when I'm as old as my father.
Which gives me until Christmas.
I simply can't cheer up —

and don't you start.
And don't you go, please, either,
till after my exercise . . .

Like skaters terrified their ice
might crack, we shuffled round
the dazzling patch of lawn

and fed each other lines:
how warm it was; how fast
the daisies grew; how difficult

low branches on an apple tree
made reaching the four corners —
anything which might slow down

the easy journey
to your room, the corridor again,
and then the glass front door.

The trouble is, I've written
scenes like this so many times
there's nothing to surprise me.

But that doesn't help one bit.
It just appals me. Now you go.
I won't come out. I'll watch you.

So you did: both hands lifted
palms out, fingers spread —
more like someone shocked

or fending something off
in passive desperation
than like someone waving –

but still clearly there,
and staring through the door
when I looked from my car,

waved back, pulled out,
then quickly vanished
down an avenue of sycamores

where glassy flecks of sunlight
skittered through the leaves, falling
blindingly along the empty street.